Grace & Giggles

A 30 Day Devotional To Brighten Your Faith Walk

LaTasha Woods

COPYRIGHT

GOLD
CROWN
PUBLISHING

INTRODUCTION

This is a journey of faith, laughter, and daily devotion! Over the next 30 days, you'll discover that spirituality doesn't have to be all serious business. In fact, sometimes the best way to connect with God is with a smile on your face and a chuckle in your heart, through the messiness of life.

Life can be a rollercoaster of ups and downs, twists and turns, and let's face it—sometimes we find ourselves hanging upside down, screaming for divine intervention! In these pages, we'll navigate the highs and lows together, armed with scripture, and a shared understanding that grace is often a lot more abundant when we can laugh at ourselves (and maybe even at the little quirks of life).

I invite you to open your heart and mind to the wisdom and wit God has in store for you. Let's embark on this adventure together, where faith, giggles, and grace blend perfectly!

TABLE OF CONTENTS

1

BLESS THIS MESS

"For God is not a God of disorder but of peace." (1 Corinthians 14:33, NIV)

Here's the truth: My life is not Pinterest-perfect. My dining room table is cluttered with last month's mail, and my closet shelf has turned into a mountain so intimidating it might qualify as a new hiking trail. Yet somehow, in the middle of all this chaos, God whispers, "I'm here."

Take yesterday, for example. I spilled coffee all over my freshly mopped floor. I'm on my hands and knees, scrubbing like I'm trying to erase a crime scene when the doorbell rings. It's the delivery guy, holding my package and grinning at my welcome mat which is now a muddy masterpiece. I laughed awkwardly, thinking, "Well, there goes the last bit of adulting credibility I had."

But here's the thing: It hit me in that moment that my life isn't supposed to look perfect for God to show up. In fact, the mess is where He does His best work.

God doesn't need spotless countertops or perfectly folded laundry to move in our lives. He works in the heart of our everyday chaos. That argument you had with your spouse?

God's in it, teaching you patience. The relentless to-do list that feels like it's crushing your soul? God's teaching you to rely on Him. The coffee stain on your shirt five minutes before your Zoom meeting? Well, maybe that's just life keeping you humble. (But hey, He's probably in that too.)

Then there are those moments that make you stop and think—like when I found a sticky note I'd written months ago with the words "God is faithful" tucked under a stack of forgotten papers. It felt like a little nudge, a reminder that He's not distant in my chaos but actively present. Maybe your sticky-note reminder is something different—a song that pops up at the right moment, a friend's encouraging text, or even the sound of laughter in your home. God's love has a funny way of slipping through the cracks when we least expect it.

Remember Martha and Mary in the Bible? Martha was running around like a stressed-out hostess, trying to make everything *just right* for Jesus. Meanwhile, Mary was chilling at His feet, soaking in His presence. And guess what? Jesus told Martha that Mary had chosen the better part. Not the perfectly set table or the spotless house... just being with Him.

Here's what I'm learning: Maybe you're like me, trying to bless your mess with another "get your life together" spree. But what if God's blessing isn't about fixing the chaos, but finding Him right in the middle of it?

Take a deep breath. Look around at your mess, literally or metaphorically, and know that God is there. Maybe your laundry pile won't magically disappear (trust me, I've prayed for that miracle), but your soul can find peace in knowing that your worth isn't in what you've cleaned up—it's in the God who loves you as you are.

It's okay if life feels overwhelming. Just remember, God's specialty is turning messes into miracles. If He can bring order to the chaos of creation, He can handle your messy Monday.

Prayer:

Lord, thank You for showing up in the middle of my mess. Help me to see You in the chaos of my life and remind me that Your peace is not dependent on my circumstances. Teach me to rest in Your presence and to trust that You're working even when life feels overwhelming. Amen.

2

HOLY COFFEE

"I can do all this through Him who gives me strength." (Philippians 4:13, NIV)

Mornings and I have an understanding when I am really tired and struggling. They don't overwhelm me, and I promise not to run back to bed after the third alarm. But let's be real: without coffee, I'm about as functional as a car without gas. It's not that I worship my coffee mug, but the sight of it steaming on the counter feels like the warm hug I need to face the day. And you know what? I think God understands.

Picture this: the disciples sitting around a fire early in the morning, groggy and maybe a little grumpy. I imagine Peter, rubbing his eyes, muttering something about fishing all night. Maybe John's looking for some leftover bread, wishing someone had invented a cappuccino machine. Even back then, people needed a moment to gear up for the day ahead. Today, coffee just happens to be part of our preparation.

But here's the thing: coffee alone doesn't cut it. Sure, it gets me moving, but it's the time I spend with God that gets my spirit going. Just like that caffeine boost for your body, spending a few moments in prayer or reading Scripture is the spiritual energy shot your soul craves. It's not about the perfect morning routine (trust me, mine is far from Pinterest-worthy). It's about inviting God into your day before the chaos takes over.

I remember one particularly hectic morning, my to-do list was already miles long when I realized I'd forgotten to restock coffee filters. Panic set in (because instant coffee wasn't an option), and I found myself saying, "Lord, help me!" It wasn't a fancy prayer, but it was real. And you know what? That little moment reminded me that God doesn't need eloquent words. He just needs an open heart.

It's easy to rush through mornings, gulping coffee while scrolling through emails, but what if we paused? Not for hours, but for a minute to say, "God, I need You today." That's where the real strength comes from—not the caffeine, but the Creator.

So tomorrow, when you pour your coffee, let it remind you of something deeper. Just like you need that first sip to wake up, your soul needs God to truly face the day. And if you're not a coffee drinker, no worries. Tea, hot chocolate, or even water works just as well. The point isn't what's in the cup; it's who fills your spirit.

Prayer:

Lord, thank You for mornings and for the little things that help us start our day. As I take my first sip of coffee (or whatever I drink), remind me to seek You first. Give me strength for the tasks ahead and peace in knowing You're with me every step of the way. Amen.

3

JESUS, TAKE THE WHEEL (AND THE GPS)

"Trust in the Lord with all your heart and lean not on your own understanding; in all your ways submit to Him, and He will make your paths straight."
(Proverbs 3:5-6, NIV)

There's nothing like a wrong turn to remind you how much you need divine intervention. I once found myself on a back road so sketchy I half-expected a tumbleweed to roll across my windshield. It was dark, my GPS signal was gone, and my phone battery was hanging on by a thread. I muttered, "Jesus, take the wheel... and maybe the GPS too?"

Life can feel like that sometimes, can't it? Like you're driving down a road you've never seen, with no idea where you're headed. You think you've got it all planned out, but then—bam!—detours, potholes, and dead ends come out of nowhere. It's frustrating, scary, and a little humbling.

But here's the thing: when we surrender control, God steps in as the ultimate navigator. His map might not look like ours, but it's always better. Where we see confusion, He sees the bigger picture. Where we see delay, He sees preparation.

6

I think of Paul in the Bible. He had plans, big ones. But God had different plans that took him places he never expected—prison cells, shipwrecks, and trials. Yet through it all, Paul trusted God's direction. He didn't always know the why or the how, but he trusted the Who.

So, the next time you're lost—literally or figuratively—remember that God doesn't need a GPS signal. He knows exactly where you're going and how to get you there. You might hit a few potholes along the way, but those bumps are just part of the journey.

Prayer:

Lord, when I feel lost or uncertain, help me to trust Your guidance. Remind me that Your plans are always better than mine, and give me peace as I follow where You lead. Amen.

4

PROCRASTINATION: THE FINE ART OF DELAYING YOUR BLESSINGS

"The soul of the sluggard craves and gets nothing,
while the soul of the diligent is richly supplied."
(Proverbs 13:4, ESV)

Ah, procrastination. If it were an Olympic sport, there are probably some people you know who could have a gold medal by now. You know that thing where you have a deadline looming, but suddenly, reorganizing your sock drawer feels like the most urgent task in the world? Yep, that's them.

But procrastination isn't just about putting off chores or work. Sometimes, it's about delaying the things God has called us to do. Maybe it's forgiving someone who hurt us, starting that Bible study we've been avoiding, or stepping out in faith on a project He's placed on our hearts. We tell ourselves, "I'll get to it tomorrow," but tomorrow turns into next week, and next week turns into... well, you get the idea.

I had a moment like this recently. I felt God nudging me to call a friend I hadn't spoken to in months. Life had gotten busy, and I kept telling myself, "I'll call her when things settle down." Spoiler alert: life didn't settle down. Finally, one evening, I picked up the phone. That conversation ended up being exactly what both of us needed—she was going through something tough, and my call was a reminder that she wasn't alone. Imagine if I had waited even longer.

The Bible has a lot to say about diligence and action. Proverbs 13:4 doesn't mince words: "The soul of the sluggard craves and gets nothing, while the soul of the diligent is richly supplied." Ouch. But it's true. When we put off what God is calling us to do, we miss out on the blessings He has in store.

Here's the good news: God's grace is bigger than our procrastination. Even when we drag our feet, He's patient with us. But imagine how much more we could experience if we said "yes" to Him today instead of tomorrow. It's not about being perfect; it's about being willing.

So, what's that one thing you've been putting off? Maybe it's reaching out to a friend, starting a new habit, or spending more time in prayer. Whatever it is, take a step today. Even if it's small, it's a step in the right direction.

Prayer:

Lord, forgive me for the times I've delayed doing what You've called me to do. Give me the courage and motivation to take action today, trusting that You'll be with me every step of the way. Help me to embrace diligence and to trust in Your timing. Amen.

5

FORGIVENESS: THE ULTIMATE RESET BUTTON (BECAUSE WHO'S PERFECT?)

"Bear with each other and forgive one another if any of you has a grievance against someone. Forgive as the Lord forgave you." (Colossians 3:13, NIV)

Forgiveness. Just hearing the word can make you cringe a little, right? It's one of those things that's easy to preach but so much harder to practice. Let's be real: forgiving someone who hurt you can feel like trying to hug a cactus. Painful, awkward, and, honestly, who wants to do it?

I'll never forget the time I had an argument with a close friend. We'd been tight for years, but one careless comment during a tough season sent our friendship into a nosedive. I felt betrayed and hurt, and I was *not* about to let it go. I carried that grudge like a badge of honor, replaying the scene in my head and coming up with all the clever comebacks I wish I'd said. (Don't act like you've never done that!)

But here's the thing about grudges: they're heavy. It didn't take long before the weight of my unforgiveness started spilling

10

over into other areas of my life. I was cranky, distracted at work, and, let's be honest, completely drained. That's when God hit me with a truth I couldn't ignore: holding onto bitterness wasn't punishing my friend—it was punishing *me*.

The Bible makes it clear: forgiveness isn't optional. Colossians 3:13 says, "Bear with each other and forgive one another if any of you has a grievance against someone. Forgive as the Lord forgave you." Did you catch that last part? Forgive as the Lord forgave you. That's a tall order, especially when you think about how much grace God has shown us. I mean, how many times have we messed up and gone running back to Him, only to find His arms wide open?

So, I took a deep breath and called my friend. I'd love to tell you it was a picture-perfect moment with violins playing in the background, but honestly, it was awkward. My voice shook, and I fumbled through my words. But you know what? It was worth it. That conversation didn't just reset our friendship; it reset my heart.

Forgiveness doesn't mean forgetting or pretending the hurt didn't happen. It's about choosing to let go of the bitterness and entrusting the situation to God. It's about freeing yourself from the prison of resentment so you can experience the peace and joy God wants for you.

Maybe you're holding onto something right now. A hurtful comment, a broken promise, or a betrayal that cut deep. Friend, it's time to hit the reset button. Not because the other person deserves it, but because *you* do. Forgiveness is a gift you give yourself—a chance to heal, move forward, and let God take the reins.

Prayer:

Lord, thank You for the incredible grace You've shown me time and time again. Help me to forgive others as You've forgiven me. When the hurt feels too big, remind me that Your love is bigger. Heal my heart and guide me as I let go of bitterness and embrace the freedom that comes with forgiveness. Amen.

HEAVENLY LAUNDRY:
SORTING OUT YOUR BAGGAGE

"Cast all your anxiety on Him because He cares for you." (1 Peter 5:7, NIV)

Laundry. The never-ending, soul-draining task that somehow multiplies when you're not looking. I'm convinced my laundry basket is in cahoots with my to-do list. Just when I think I've caught up, I find another pile lurking in the shadows. Sound familiar?

Here's the thing about laundry—it's not just clothes we're sorting through. It's life. Each item in that basket could symbolize something we've been carrying around for way too long. The stained t-shirt? That's the guilt we keep revisiting. The mismatched socks? Those are the relationships we can't quite figure out. And the wrinkled blouse at the bottom? That's the anxiety we've been shoving down, hoping it will magically disappear.

I was reminded of a scene from a movie where the main character opens their closet, only to be buried under an avalanche of clothes they haven't worn in years. One item in particular—a worn-out sweater—holds a deep emotional attachment. It symbolizes a time when they felt rejected and insecure, and they struggle to let it go. The moment is poignant because it mirrors how we often hold onto things that weigh us down, both physically and emotionally. Watching that character finally take a deep breath and toss the sweater away was a nudge for me—a reminder of God's gentle call to release the baggage we've been clinging to.

The Bible tells us in 1 Peter 5:7, "Cast all your anxiety on Him because He cares for you." That word "cast" isn't a gentle suggestion; it's an action. It's like tossing your dirty laundry into the washer and trusting that it will come out clean. But here's the catch: you have to let go of it first. You can't wash what you're still holding onto.

Sometimes, we're like those people who refuse to part with an old, tattered hoodie because it's "comfortable." We'd rather cling to our baggage—our fears, regrets, and wounds—because dealing with them feels too overwhelming. But God doesn't want us to lug around those burdens. He wants us to hand them over to Him and trust that He'll take care of them.

Imagine if you brought all your dirty laundry to the laundromat, but instead of putting it in the washer, you just sat there holding it. Sounds ridiculous, right? Yet that's what we do when we try to carry our baggage instead of giving it to God. We sit in our mess, wondering why we feel so weighed down, when all along, God is saying, "Give it to Me. Let Me clean it up."

So, what's in your "laundry basket" right now? Maybe it's worry about the future, guilt over past mistakes, or frustration with someone who's hurt you. Whatever it is, you don't have to carry it alone. Toss it to God. Let Him sort it out, clean it up, and show you that His grace is more than enough.

Prayer:

Lord, thank You for caring about every detail of my life, even the messy ones. Help me to cast my burdens on You and trust that You'll handle them with love and grace. Teach me to let go of the things I've been holding onto and to rest in the freedom that comes from Your peace. Amen.

7

MIRACLES IN THE MICROWAVE: FINDING FAITH IN FAST FOOD

"Be still, and know that I am God." (Psalm 46:10, NIV)

We live in a fast-paced, microwave society. Everything—from our meals to our internet connections—has to be quick, convenient, and ready the moment we want it. And while there's nothing wrong with heating up leftovers or ordering takeout on a busy night, sometimes this instant-gratification mindset sneaks into our faith life.

Take my last attempt at cooking, for example. I had grand plans of preparing a hearty meal from scratch. I chopped vegetables, marinated meat, and followed the recipe step by step. But halfway through, I got impatient. It was taking too long, and my stomach started growling louder than my prayers. So, I abandoned the stove and popped a frozen meal into the microwave. Three minutes later, dinner was served. Was it gourmet? Not even close. But it was fast, and that's what I thought I needed.

Faith doesn't work like that. You can't microwave your way through spiritual growth, prayers, or trust in God. The truth is, some of God's best work happens while we're waiting—in the slow cooker moments of life when we'd rather speed things up.

In Psalm 46:10, God says, "Be still, and know that I am God." Be still. Not "be productive," not "hustle harder," not "push for instant answers." Just be still. And let's be honest: being still is hard. We like results. We like solutions. We like knowing what's coming next. But faith isn't about knowing the whole plan; it's about trusting the One who holds it.

I had a "microwave moment" not long ago when I prayed for an answer about a big decision. I wanted clarity, and I wanted it *now*. But days turned into weeks, and it felt like God was on mute. Frustrated, I asked Him, "Why aren't You answering me?" And that's when I felt His gentle nudge: "I am answering. You just need to wait."

Waiting is where trust grows. It's where God refines us, shapes us, and teaches us to rely on Him instead of our own timelines. Think about all the biblical greats who had to wait: Abraham waited for God's promise of a son. Joseph waited years in prison before stepping into his destiny. Even Jesus spent 40 days in the wilderness before beginning His ministry. Their waiting wasn't wasted. It was part of God's greater plan.

So, the next time you find yourself wishing you could zap your way through a tough situation, remember this: God's timing is always perfect. He's never late, never rushed, and never working on autopilot. Trust that He's preparing something far better than anything you could cook up on your own.

Prayer:

Lord, thank You for reminding me that waiting is never wasted when You're in control. Help me to trust Your timing and to find peace in the stillness. Teach me to let go of my impatience and to embrace the slow, beautiful work You're doing in my life. Amen.

8

GOD'S GYM: SPIRITUAL WORKOUTS THAT DON'T REQUIRE SPANDEX

"For physical training is of some value, but godliness has value for all things, holding promise for both the present life and the life to come." (1 Timothy 4:8, NIV)

Confession time: I'm not a fan of the gym. The thought of running on a treadmill or doing endless squats makes me want to hide under a blanket with a chocolate bar, but I have friends who swear by their gym routines. They'll tell you that while the workouts are tough, the results are worth it. And you know what? They're right. Growth, whether physical or spiritual, requires effort.

Thankfully, God's gym doesn't involve burpees or spandex—unless you're into that sort of thing. Instead, it's about strengthening our faith muscles through trust, obedience, and perseverance. And just like in a physical gym, spiritual workouts aren't always easy, but they're essential for growth.

There used to be a teacher who faced incredible betrayal from a close friend. Rather than retaliate or harbor resentment, the teacher chose to extend grace over time, even though it was difficult. Each effort to rebuild the relationship, felt like lifting a heavy weight—slow and challenging. Yet, with each step of forgiveness, they found more freedom and peace. It was a testament to how God empowers us to let go of bitterness and rely on His strength to move forward, one act of grace at a time.

In 1 Timothy 4:8, Paul writes, "For physical training is of some value, but godliness has value for all things, holding promise for both the present life and the life to come." Think about that. While it's great to have a healthy body, a strong faith carries eternal benefits. It equips us to handle life's challenges, love others well, and reflect God's goodness in a world that desperately needs it.

So, what does a spiritual workout look like? Maybe it's choosing to pray instead of worrying. Maybe it's spending time in God's Word when you'd rather binge-watch your favorite show. Maybe it's showing kindness to someone who doesn't deserve it. Each of these acts stretches and strengthens our faith, just like lifting weights builds muscle.

Here's the thing about God's gym: you don't have to go it alone. The Holy Spirit is your personal trainer, guiding and encouraging you every step of the way. And the best part? There's no membership fee. Jesus already paid it in full.

So, the next time you face a challenge or feel stretched beyond your limits, remember that it's all part of the workout. God is using it to build your faith, refine your character, and draw you closer to Him. And while it might feel tough in the moment, the results—peace, joy, and a stronger relationship with God—are more than worth it.

Prayer:

Lord, thank You for being my strength when I feel weak. Help me to embrace the spiritual workouts You place in my life, knowing that they're shaping me into who You've called me to be. Remind me to rely on Your power and not my own, and give me the perseverance to keep going even when it's hard. Amen.

PRAYER: TEXTING THE DIVINE—ARE YOU ON DO NOT DISTURB?

"The Lord is near to all who call on him, to all who call on him in truth." (Psalm 145:18, ESV)

Imagine this: you send a text to your best friend, pouring your heart out about something important, and then you wait, and wait. But the reply never comes. You check your phone, only to realize… you were on Do Not Disturb the whole time! How frustrating, right?

Now flip the scenario. What if we're the ones putting God on Do Not Disturb? We might not do it intentionally, but let's be honest—how often do we push prayer to the bottom of our priority list because we're "too busy" or "too distracted"? Yet, the beautiful thing about God is that He's always ready to listen. He never leaves us on read or sends us straight to voicemail.

Prayer is our direct line to the Creator of the universe. Think about that for a second. The One who spoke galaxies into existence invites *you* to talk to Him. You don't need the perfect words, a fancy setting, or even a solid Wi-Fi connection. He's near to all who call on Him (Psalm 145:18). The only requirement? Sincerity.

I remember a season when my prayers felt more like monologues. I would rattle off a list of requests, say a quick "Amen," and move on with my day. It was like sending a text without waiting for a response. Prayer isn't meant to be a one-sided conversation. It's a dialogue. And sometimes, the most powerful part of prayer is simply sitting in God's presence and listening.

Take Jesus as our example. Despite His busy schedule of preaching, healing, and performing miracles, He consistently made time to pray. He would withdraw to quiet places, not just to ask for things but to commune with His Father. If the Son of God prioritized prayer, how much more should we?

But let's face it: prayer isn't always easy. Life gets noisy. Distractions creep in. Some days, it feels like our words are bouncing off the ceiling. During those moments, remember this: prayer isn't about getting it "right." It's about being real. He hears you, whether you're whispering a desperate plea in your car or silently thanking God as you drift off to sleep.

So, how do we take God off Do Not Disturb? Start small. Set aside five minutes in the morning to talk to Him. Write your prayers in a journal. Turn off the noise—literally and figuratively—and focus on His presence. You might be surprised at how your relationship with Him deepens.

Remember, God isn't waiting for perfect prayers. He's waiting for *you*. And the best part? When you call on Him, you'll never hear, "I'll get back to you later."

Prayer:

Lord, thank You for always being near and ready to listen. Forgive me for the times I've put You on hold or let distractions get in the way. Help me to make prayer a priority and to approach You with honesty and faith. Teach me to listen for Your voice and to trust in Your timing. Amen.

10

HUMILITY: LEARNING TO BOW WITHOUT BUMPING YOUR HEAD

"Humble yourselves before the Lord, and He will lift you up." (James 4:10, NIV)

Humility is tricky, isn't it? The moment you think you've got it, you've probably already lost it. It's like trying to balance on one leg while juggling—if you focus too much on the act, you're likely to fall. And let's be real: in a world where self-promotion and "standing out" are celebrated, humility often feels countercultural. But God's kingdom operates on an upside-down principle: the way up is down.

I learned this the hard way when I decided to take on a leadership role at church. I was excited, confident, and maybe... just a little bit full of myself. I mean, how hard could it be? I'd read the books, watched the tutorials, and even had a catchy vision statement ready to go. But a few weeks in, I hit a wall—hard. Nothing was going as planned. Projects were delayed, miscommunications piled up, and I found myself overwhelmed. One day, as I sat in frustration, God whispered something I'll never forget: "It's not about you."

Ouch. That one hit deep, but it was exactly what I needed to hear. I had been so focused on my ideas and my goals that I'd forgotten the true purpose of serving: glorifying God, not myself.

The Bible is full of reminders about humility. James 4:10 says, "Humble yourselves before the Lord, and He will lift you up." Notice the order here. We humble ourselves first, and then God does the lifting. It's not about tearing ourselves down or pretending we're unworthy. It's about recognizing that every good thing we have comes from Him and giving Him the credit.

Jesus modeled this perfectly. Philippians 2:6-7 tells us that although He was in the very nature of God, He didn't cling to His divine status. Instead, He humbled Himself, taking on the nature of a servant. Think about that: the Creator of the universe chose to wash feet, touch lepers, and hang out with outcasts. If He can do that, what excuse do we have?

So, how do we practice humility without turning it into a performance? Here are a few ideas:

1. **Celebrate Others:** Instead of focusing on your own achievements, cheer on those around you. Genuine encouragement goes a long way.

2. **Serve Quietly:** Do something kind without expecting recognition. Maybe it's washing dishes, helping a neighbor, or sending an anonymous gift.

3. **Admit Mistakes:** This one's tough but powerful. When you mess up, own it. Apologize sincerely and learn from it.

Humility isn't about thinking less of yourself; it's about thinking of yourself less. It's about bowing low so God can lift you high in His time and His way. And trust me, when He does the lifting, it's always worth it.

Prayer:

Lord, thank You for showing me the beauty of humility through Your Son, Jesus. Help me to keep my focus on You and to serve with a heart that seeks Your glory, not my own. Teach me to celebrate others, admit my mistakes, and trust in Your timing. Lift me up according to Your perfect will. Amen.

11

FAITHFUL FITNESS: RUNNING THE RACE WITHOUT LOSING YOUR BREATH (OR MIND)

"Do you not know that in a race all the runners run, but only one gets the prize? Run in such a way as to get the prize." (1 Corinthians 9:24, NIV)

The Christian life is often compared to a race, but it's not a sprint. It's a marathon—one that requires perseverance, discipline, and a clear focus on the finish line. Unlike a physical race, where the goal is to cross the finish line first, our spiritual race is about running faithfully and finishing well.

Paul's words in 1 Corinthians 9:24 remind us to run with purpose. Just as an athlete trains rigorously to compete, we are called to live intentionally for God, setting aside distractions and anything that hinders our progress. Training for a marathon requires more than good intentions; it demands commitment, endurance, and the right mindset. Similarly, our spiritual growth doesn't happen by accident. It requires us to stay disciplined in prayer, study God's Word, and live out our faith daily.

The truth is, the race isn't always easy. There are times when the path feels uphill, the wind is against us, and we're tempted to give up. But the good news is that we're not running alone. God is our ultimate coach, providing strength when we're weak and cheering us on when we feel like quitting. Isaiah 40:31 says, "But those who hope in the Lord will renew their strength. They will soar on wings like eagles; they will run and not grow weary, they will walk and not be faint." (NIV) His promise is clear: when we rely on Him, He will sustain us.

In every race, there are also moments of joy—those times when we see the fruit of our faith and realize how far we've come. Maybe it's a restored relationship, an answered prayer, or simply the peace of knowing we're walking in God's will. These moments remind us why we keep going and encourage us to press on.

But how do we stay faithful in this race? Here are three practical tips:

1. **Stay Focused on the Goal:** Hebrews 12:1-2 encourages us to "run with perseverance the race marked out for us, fixing our eyes on Jesus." When we keep our focus on Him, distractions fade, and our purpose becomes clear.

2. **Run at Your Own Pace:** Comparison is a trap. Your race won't look like anyone else's, and that's okay. God has a unique plan for your life, so stay in your lane and trust His timing.

3. **Rest When Needed:** Even the strongest runners need to refuel. Take time to rest in God's presence, allowing Him to refresh your spirit and renew your strength.

Remember, the prize isn't about earthly accolades or achievements; it's about hearing these words at the finish line:

"Well done, good and faithful servant" (Matthew 25:21). Keep running, keep trusting, and keep your eyes on Jesus. The race is worth it.

Prayer:

Lord, thank You for calling me to run this race of faith. Give me the strength to persevere, the focus to keep my eyes on You, and the discipline to stay faithful. Help me to run with purpose and to trust in Your plan, even when the journey feels hard. Thank You for being my source of strength and for cheering me on every step of the way. Amen.

12

GRATITUDE: THE SECRET SAUCE FOR A HAPPY HEART

"Give thanks in all circumstances; for this is God's will for you in Christ Jesus." (1 Thessalonians 5:18, NIV)

Gratitude is a lot like seasoning. Without it, life can feel bland, even when everything seems to be going right. But with it, even the smallest things—a morning sunrise, a kind word, or a good night's sleep—can bring immense joy and flavor to our lives. Gratitude shifts our perspective from what's missing to what's present, and that shift changes everything.

The Bible tells us to "give thanks in all circumstances" (1 Thessalonians 5:18). Notice it doesn't say to give thanks *for* all circumstances but *in* them. That's a big difference. It's not about pretending everything is perfect or denying life's challenges. It's about finding something to be grateful for, even in the middle of the mess.

Take the Israelites, for example. After God delivered them from slavery in Egypt, they had every reason to be thankful. Yet, as they wandered through the wilderness, gratitude quickly turned into grumbling. They complained about food, water, and even the journey itself. It's easy to judge them, but if we're honest, we do the same thing. How often do we overlook God's blessings because we're too focused on what we think is missing?

Gratitude isn't just about saying "thank you" to God; it's about cultivating a mindset of appreciation. It's about waking up each day and choosing to see His fingerprints in our lives. It's about recognizing that the very breath in our lungs is a gift we didn't earn but freely received. And the more we practice gratitude, the more it becomes a natural part of who we are.

Practicing gratitude doesn't require grand gestures. It can be as simple as keeping a gratitude journal, where you jot down three things you're thankful for each day. Or taking a moment during your prayers to thank God for specific blessings. Over time, you'll find that these small acts create a big shift in your heart.

Gratitude also has a ripple effect. When we express thankfulness, it not only deepens our relationship with God but also encourages those around us. A simple "thank you" can brighten someone's day and remind them of God's goodness. In a world that often highlights negativity, gratitude is a powerful testimony of faith.

So, what are you grateful for today? Maybe it's something as small as the sound of birds outside your window or as big as a prayer that was recently answered. Whatever it is, take a moment to thank God for it. And as you do, watch how gratitude transforms your heart and fills it with His joy.

Prayer:

Lord, thank You for the countless blessings You've poured into my life. Forgive me for the times I've taken them for granted or focused on what I lack. Teach me to have a heart of gratitude in every circumstance, knowing that You are always good and always faithful. Help me to be a source of encouragement to others, reflecting Your love and goodness. Amen.

13

THE FRUIT OF THE SPIRIT: NO SPOILING ALLOWED!

"But the fruit of the Spirit is love, joy, peace, forbearance, kindness, goodness, faithfulness, gentleness and self-control. Against such things there is no law." (Galatians 5:22-23, NIV)

The phrase "fruit of the Spirit" paints such a vibrant and inviting picture. Unlike the apples and bananas on your kitchen counter, the fruit of the Spirit doesn't rot or spoil—at least, not if we stay rooted in Christ. These attributes are evidence of a life transformed by the Holy Spirit. They're not things we achieve through sheer willpower; they grow in us as we abide in Him.

Think about fruit for a moment. It doesn't grow overnight. It requires the right conditions—sunlight, water, good soil, and time. Similarly, the fruit of the Spirit develops in us through daily dependence on God. Love, joy, peace, and the rest don't magically appear. They are cultivated as we walk with Him, learn from Him, and allow Him to prune the areas in our lives that hinder growth.

Jesus says in John 15:5, "I am the vine; you are the branches. If you remain in me and I in you, you will bear much fruit; apart from me you can do nothing" (NIV). Remaining in Him means keeping a close connection through prayer, studying Scripture, and obeying His commands. Without that connection, we risk becoming spiritually dry and unproductive—like a branch cut off from its vine.

But let's be honest: producing spiritual fruit isn't always easy. Love can be hard when people are unkind. Joy can feel distant in the midst of trials. Peace seems elusive when life gets chaotic. And self-control? Well, let's just say it's tested every time someone cuts you off in traffic. That's why it's so important to rely on the Holy Spirit. He empowers us to grow these fruits even when circumstances make it difficult.

As we grow, the fruit of the Spirit isn't just for our benefit— it's also for others. Think of how a tree doesn't eat its own fruit. Its fruit exists to nourish those around it. In the same way, our love, kindness, patience, and other spiritual fruits bless and encourage the people in our lives, pointing them to the God who produces such goodness in us.

So, take a moment to reflect: how's your spiritual fruit looking? Are there areas where growth feels slow or stalled? If so, don't be discouraged. Growth takes time, and God is patient. As you remain in Him, He will continue His work in you, producing fruit that is vibrant, life-giving, and eternal.

Prayer:

Lord, thank You for the work You're doing in my heart, producing fruit that reflects Your character. Help me to remain connected to You, trusting that You will continue to cultivate love, joy, peace, and all the other fruits of the Spirit in my life.

Teach me to rely on Your strength and not my own, and use my life to bless those around me. Amen.

14

WAITING ON GOD: THE PATIENCE GAME—ARE WE THERE YET?

"Wait for the Lord; be strong and take heart and wait for the Lord." (Psalm 27:14, NIV)

Waiting is hard. Whether it's waiting for your coffee to brew, for a long line to move, or for God to answer a heartfelt prayer, the act of waiting can test even the most patient among us. In our fast-paced world, where instant gratification is often just a click away, waiting feels unnatural—even unbearable. Yet, God calls us to wait, not with frustration, but with trust.

David's words in Psalm 27:14 remind us of the strength and courage required to wait on the Lord. Waiting isn't a passive act; it's an active display of faith. It's choosing to believe that God's timing is perfect, even when it doesn't align with our own. It's trusting that His delays are not denials but opportunities for growth and preparation.

Think of Abraham and Sarah. God promised them a child, but that promise took years to be fulfilled. In their waiting, they experienced doubt, impatience, and even tried to take matters into their own hands. Yet, God remained faithful, and Isaac was born at just the right time. Their story reminds us that God's promises are worth the wait, no matter how long it takes.

Waiting on God often feels like standing still while the world moves on without you. But the truth is, God is never idle in our waiting. He is working behind the scenes, orchestrating circumstances, aligning opportunities, and shaping us into who we need to be. Sometimes, the waiting season is less about what we're waiting for and more about what God is doing in us.

In the waiting, we learn patience. We learn to lean on God instead of our own understanding. We learn to surrender our timelines and embrace His. And as hard as it may be, waiting is where our faith is refined and our trust in God deepens.

But how do we wait well? The key is to stay connected to God during the process. Pray for strength and clarity. Dive into His Word for reassurance and hope. Surround yourself with people who will encourage you and remind you of His faithfulness. Waiting is easier when we're anchored in Him.

If you're in a season of waiting, take heart. God sees you. He knows your desires, your struggles, and your frustrations. He is not ignoring you; He is preparing something better than you can imagine. And when the time is right, His answer will come—and it will be worth every moment you spent waiting.

Prayer:

Lord, waiting is hard, but I trust in Your perfect timing. Help me to be patient and to focus on what You're teaching me during this season. Strengthen my faith and remind me of Your promises. Thank You for working behind the scenes and for the blessings You have in store. I choose to trust You as I wait. Amen.

15

BLESSINGS IN DISGUISE: FINDING GOLD IN YOUR DAILY GRIND

"And we know that in all things God works for the good of those who love Him, who have been called according to His purpose." (Romans 8:28, NIV)

Life is full of daily tasks that feel mundane. Laundry, grocery shopping, commuting to work—these activities rarely seem like the backdrop for God's greatest blessings. Yet, the beauty of God's plan is that He often uses the ordinary to accomplish the extraordinary. What if the moments you see as trivial are the very places where God is shaping you, growing you, and revealing His blessings?

Romans 8:28 reminds us of a powerful truth: God works in *all things* for our good. Not just the exciting moments or the obvious blessings, but the small, unremarkable parts of life too. The challenge is to have eyes that see and hearts that trust, even when the blessings don't look like what we expected.

Think about the story of Ruth. Her life seemed ordinary, even tragic. A widow in a foreign land, she spent her days gleaning

40

leftover grain just to survive. Yet, in that daily grind, God was weaving a story of redemption and blessing. Through her faithfulness in the small things, Ruth became part of the lineage of Jesus. What looked like a season of struggle was actually a setup for God's greater purpose.

The same principle applies to us. Maybe you're in a job that feels unfulfilling or juggling responsibilities that leave you drained. It's easy to think, "How could God possibly be at work here?" He is. Sometimes, His blessings come disguised as lessons in patience, opportunities to serve, or moments to grow closer to Him. Often, it's not until we look back that we realize the gold hidden in our daily grind.

The key is to approach each day with a heart of gratitude and faith. Instead of asking, "Why do I have to do this?" try asking, "Lord, what are You teaching me through this?" That shift in perspective can turn frustration into worship and routine into revelation. It helps us see that nothing in God's plan is wasted.

Blessings in disguise also teach us to trust God's bigger picture. We may not understand why certain things happen, but we can rest in the truth that He is working for our good and His glory. Just as gold is refined through fire, our character and faith are refined through the challenges and routines of life. These are the moments where God molds us into vessels ready to carry His blessings.

So today, take a moment to reflect on the ordinary parts of your life. Ask God to open your eyes to the hidden blessings and to give you the faith to trust in His purpose. You might just discover that the gold you've been searching for has been right in front of you all along.

Prayer:

41

Lord, thank You for working in all things, even the ones that seem ordinary or difficult. Help me to see the blessings in my daily life and to trust that You are using every moment for my good and Your glory. Teach me to approach each day with gratitude and faith, knowing that nothing is wasted in Your plan. Refine me through the process, and help me to find joy in the journey. Amen.

16

OVERWHELMED? JOIN THE CLUB: TIPS FROM THE BIBLE ON HANDLING LIFE'S STRESS

"Cast all your anxiety on Him because He cares for you." (1 Peter 5:7, NIV)

Feeling overwhelmed seems to be a universal experience. Whether it's work deadlines, family responsibilities, financial pressures, or just the general busyness of life, stress can pile up until it feels like too much to bear. In these moments, the Bible offers us practical and spiritual wisdom to help us navigate life's stresses.

Peter reminds us in 1 Peter 5:7 to cast our anxieties on God. The word "cast" is significant—it implies an intentional act of handing over something heavy. Imagine carrying a giant, overloaded backpack and having someone say, "Let me take that for you." That's what God invites us to do with our worries and stresses. He doesn't expect us to carry the weight of the world on our shoulders.

When we're overwhelmed, it's easy to forget that God cares deeply about every detail of our lives. Sometimes, we convince ourselves that our worries are too small or insignificant to bring to Him. But the truth is, nothing is too small for a God who numbers the hairs on our heads (Matthew 10:30). He cares about your work struggles, your family dynamics, and even the errands you're scrambling to finish.

In times of stress, it's also helpful to remember the example of Jesus. Even during His ministry, which was marked by constant demands and pressing crowds, Jesus prioritized rest and prayer. Luke 5:16 tells us that "Jesus often withdrew to lonely places and prayed." If the Son of God needed moments of stillness to recharge and reconnect with the Father, how much more do we?

The Bible also encourages us to take a step back and refocus our minds. Philippians 4:8 urges us to dwell on what is true, noble, right, pure, lovely, and admirable. When stress takes over, our minds tend to spiral into worst-case scenarios. But by shifting our focus to God's goodness and His promises, we can find peace in the chaos.

It's important to acknowledge that stress won't magically disappear, even with prayer and perspective. God equips us to face it with strength, wisdom, and grace. He may provide comfort through Scripture, encouragement from a friend, or even a quiet moment where His presence feels unmistakably real. The key is to keep seeking Him, even when life feels overwhelming.

So, if you're feeling stressed today, take a moment to pause. Breathe deeply, pray honestly, and remind yourself that you're not alone. God is with you, ready to shoulder your burdens and guide you through every challenge. Trust Him to provide the peace and strength you need to keep moving forward.

Prayer:

Lord, thank You for caring about every detail of my life. When I feel overwhelmed, help me to remember that I can cast all my anxieties on You. Teach me to trust in Your strength and to take moments to rest and refocus. Fill my heart with peace and remind me that I am never alone, no matter how heavy life feels. Amen.

17

SPIRITUAL MULTITASKING: WORRY LESS, PRAY MORE

"Do not be anxious about anything, but in every situation, by prayer and petition, with thanksgiving, present your requests to God." (Philippians 4:6, NIV)

Life can feel like a juggling act. Between work, family, errands, and everything in between, it's easy for our minds to become crowded with worry. And as much as we like to believe we're good at multitasking, the truth is, we often end up frazzled, distracted, and less productive. But what if instead of worrying and juggling everything alone, we turned our multitasking into an opportunity to connect with God?

Paul's words in Philippians 4:6 invites us to a simple yet profound shift: worry less, pray more. Instead of letting anxiety dominate our thoughts, we're encouraged to bring every concern—big or small—to God in prayer. Prayer isn't just a ritual; it's a powerful way to release our burdens and invite God into the messiness of our lives.

Here's the beauty of this practice: it doesn't require a special time, place, or posture. You can pray while folding laundry, driving to work, or even standing in line at the grocery store. It's about staying connected to God throughout your day, letting Him be part of every thought and every task.

Worry, on the other hand, is like running on a treadmill—you're exerting energy but not getting anywhere. It drains your joy and clouds your perspective. But when we choose to pray instead, we're reminded that we're not in this alone. God's peace, which surpasses all understanding, guards our hearts and minds (Philippians 4:7). That peace doesn't come from having all the answers; it comes from trusting the One who does.

The Bible is full of reminders that God is our ultimate helper and provider. Psalm 55:22 says, "Cast your cares on the Lord and He will sustain you." Jesus Himself invites us in Matthew 11:28: "Come to me, all you who are weary and burdened, and I will give you rest." These are not empty promises; they are truths we can hold onto when life feels overwhelming.

To embrace spiritual multitasking, start small. The next time you feel worry creeping in, pause and pray. It doesn't have to be long or eloquent—just honest. Something as simple as, "Lord, I'm overwhelmed. Please help me," can shift your focus from your problem to His presence. Pair your prayer with gratitude, as Paul suggests, and watch how thanksgiving transforms your outlook.

Over time, you'll find that prayer becomes less of a last resort and more of a natural rhythm. Instead of letting worry take over, you'll experience the calm assurance that comes from walking through life with God by your side. And as you juggle the demands of your day, you'll discover that His strength, not yours, is what keeps everything in balance.

Prayer:

Lord, thank You for inviting me to bring all my worries and cares to You. Teach me to turn to You in prayer instead of letting anxiety take over. Help me to trust in Your peace and provision, and remind me to stay connected to You throughout my day. Thank You for walking with me through every moment, big or small. Amen.

18

LOVE THY NEIGHBOR: ESPECIALLY WHEN THEY STEAL YOUR PARKING SPOT

"A new command I give you: Love one another. As I have loved you, so you must love one another." (John 13:34, NIV)

Loving others is easy when they're kind, thoughtful, and share your preferences. What about when they test your patience? Like, for instance, when someone swoops in and takes the parking spot you were clearly about to claim? Loving your neighbor in moments like that can feel less like a command and more like a monumental challenge.

In John 13:34, Jesus tells His disciples to love one another as He has loved them. Notice the standard: not just any kind of love, but the kind that mirrors Jesus' own. That's a high bar, considering His love is selfless, sacrificial, and unconditional. It's easy to extend love when it costs us nothing, but true Christ-like love often requires humility and grace—especially when we feel wronged.

Think of the parable of the Good Samaritan in Luke 10:25-37. A man is attacked and left for dead, and the people who should have helped him—the priest and the Levite—pass him by. But a Samaritan, someone who would have been considered an enemy, stops and shows compassion. He not only helps but goes the extra mile, ensuring the man receives care. Jesus uses this story to teach us that our "neighbor" isn't just the person we like or agree with; it's anyone we encounter, even those who challenge us.

Loving our neighbors in difficult moments requires us to let go of pride and embrace God's perspective. It's about seeing people as He sees them—flawed but valuable, just like us. That person who cut you off in traffic or left their trash in your yard? They're a child of God, too, and they're worthy of love, even if they don't seem to deserve it.

Loving your neighbor doesn't mean ignoring boundaries or excusing bad behavior. It means choosing to respond with kindness instead of anger, forgiveness instead of bitterness, and grace instead of judgment. It's about reflecting God's love in a world that often expects retaliation.

If you're struggling to love someone right now, start with prayer. Ask God to soften your heart and give you His perspective. Remember that He has shown you extraordinary grace, and He calls you to extend that grace to others. Small acts of love—a smile, a kind word, or a gesture of help—can have a ripple effect, demonstrating God's love in tangible ways.

So the next time someone steals your parking spot—or does something equally frustrating—pause and choose love. It's not always easy, but it's always worth it. In doing so, you'll not only obey Jesus' command but also reflect His love to a world that desperately needs it.

Prayer:

Lord, thank You for loving me unconditionally, even when I fall short. Help me to see others through Your eyes and to respond with grace and kindness, even when it's hard. Teach me to love my neighbors as You have loved me, and let my actions reflect Your goodness. Thank You for the opportunity to share Your love in every interaction. Amen.

19

EMBRACING YOUR QUIRKINESS: GOD MADE YOU UNIQUE—WHY FIT IN?

"For we are God's handiwork, created in Christ Jesus to do good works, which God prepared in advance for us to do." (Ephesians 2:10, NIV)

Have you ever looked in the mirror and thought, "Why am I like this?" Maybe it's your quirky laugh, your love for obscure hobbies, or the way your mind works differently from others. In a world that often celebrates conformity, being different can feel like a disadvantage. But here's the truth: your uniqueness is not a flaw; it's a feature. God made you exactly as you are for a reason.

Ephesians 2:10 reminds us that we are God's handiwork—a masterpiece, created with care and purpose. Think about that. The Creator of the universe took the time to design you, not as a carbon copy of someone else, but as a one-of-a-kind reflection of His creativity. Every quirk, talent, and trait you have is intentional, meant to serve His unique plan for your life.

It's easy to fall into the trap of comparison, especially in the age of social media. We see others' highlight reels and think, "If only I were more like them." But comparison is a thief of joy and a distraction from God's plan. When we focus on what we're not, we lose sight of who God created us to be. Psalm 139:14 says, "I praise You because I am fearfully and wonderfully made; Your works are wonderful, I know that full well." (NIV) That includes you. Your quirks, your imperfections, your uniqueness—all of it is part of God's wonderful work.

The Bible is full of people who didn't "fit in." Moses had a speech impediment, yet God used him to lead a nation. David was a shepherd boy, overlooked by everyone but chosen by God to be king. Rahab was an outsider, yet her courage placed her in the lineage of Jesus. Each of them embraced their unique place in God's story and trusted Him to use them just as they were.

Instead of trying to blend in, lean into who God made you to be. Your quirks might be the very thing that sets you apart for a specific purpose. That quirky sense of humor could brighten someone's day. Your unconventional way of thinking might solve a problem no one else can. Your quiet nature could create a safe space for someone who needs to be heard. God doesn't waste anything, including the traits that make you different.

So, the next time you catch yourself wishing you were "normal," remember this: normal is overrated. God didn't call you to fit in; He called you to stand out. Embrace your uniqueness, and let Him use it for His glory.

Prayer:

Lord, thank You for making me uniquely and wonderfully. Forgive me for the times I've doubted Your design or tried to be someone I'm not. Help me to embrace the person You've created me to be and to use my quirks and gifts to glorify You. Teach me to trust in Your purpose and to celebrate the uniqueness of others as well. Amen.

20

THE ARMOR OF GOD: BECAUSE LIFE IS LIKE A VIDEO GAME

"Put on the full armor of God, so that you can take your stand against the devil's schemes." (Ephesians 6:11, NIV)

If you've ever played a video game, you know that before you face a tough level or boss, you make sure your character is equipped with the best armor and weapons. You don't go into battle unprepared because you know the enemy is waiting to strike. Life isn't so different. Every day, we face challenges, temptations, and spiritual battles that test our faith. Thankfully, God has given us everything we need to stand strong—His armor.

Ephesians 6:11 calls us to put on the full armor of God. This isn't just a suggestion; it's a command for our spiritual survival. Paul, the author of Ephesians, uses the metaphor of armor to help us understand the spiritual tools God provides. Each piece has a specific purpose, and when we wear it all, we're equipped to face whatever comes our way.

First, there's the belt of truth. In a world full of deception and half-truths, God's truth is our foundation. It holds everything together and keeps us grounded in His Word. Then there's the breastplate of righteousness, which protects our hearts from guilt, shame, and the lies of the enemy. We're reminded that our righteousness comes from Christ, not from our own efforts.

The shoes of peace prepare us to stand firm and to share the Gospel wherever we go. Life is full of chaos, but God's peace gives us stability. The shield of faith is our defense against the enemy's fiery darts—those doubts, fears, and temptations that threaten to derail us. With faith, we can extinguish them and stay on course.

Next is the helmet of salvation, which guards our minds. Our thoughts can be a battlefield, but when we remember that we are saved and secure in Christ, we can combat negativity and lies. Finally, there's the sword of the Spirit, which is the Word of God. It's our offensive weapon, allowing us to counter lies and attack with the truth of Scripture.

But putting on this armor isn't a one-time event. It's a daily practice. Just as you wouldn't go into a video game battle without preparing, you can't face life's challenges without equipping yourself spiritually. Prayer is your strategy guide, helping you stay connected to God and reminding you to rely on His strength, not your own.

When you feel overwhelmed by life's battles, remember that you're not fighting alone. God has already equipped you with everything you need to stand firm. You just have to put it on. And the best part? In Christ, the victory is already won.

Prayer:

Lord, thank You for giving me Your armor to face life's challenges. Help me to put it on daily and to trust in Your strength rather than my own. Remind me that I am not fighting alone and that You have already secured the victory. Guide my thoughts, guard my heart, and fill me with peace as I stand firm in You. Amen.

21

CRAZY FAMILY TIES: FINDING GRACE AMONG THE CHAOS

"If it is possible, as far as it depends on you, live at peace with everyone." (Romans 12:18, NIV)

Families are beautiful, messy, and often complicated. They bring us joy and, at times, test our patience. Whether it's the sibling who knows exactly how to push your buttons, the uncle with strong opinions, or the parent who struggles to understand your choices, navigating family dynamics can feel like walking a tightrope.

The Bible doesn't shy away from the reality of messy families. Just look at Joseph and his brothers. Jealousy led to betrayal, and Joseph found himself sold into slavery by the very people who should have protected him. Yet, through God's grace, their story didn't end there. In Genesis 50:20, Joseph says to his brothers, "You intended to harm me, but God intended it for good." That's the beauty of God's work—He can bring restoration and purpose even to the most fractured relationships.

Romans 12:18 encourages us to live at peace with everyone, as far as it depends on us. That phrase, "as far as it depends on you," is key. While we can't control how others act, we can control our own responses. We can choose grace over grudges, kindness over criticism, and love over division. Living at peace doesn't mean avoiding conflict or pretending problems don't exist; it means approaching challenges with a heart committed to reconciliation and understanding.

But let's be real: loving our family isn't always easy. Sometimes, the people closest to us can hurt us the most. In those moments, forgiveness becomes essential. Forgiveness doesn't excuse wrong behavior or erase pain, but it frees us from bitterness and opens the door for healing. It's a reflection of God's grace, which He freely gives to us and calls us to extend to others.

Practical grace within families starts with small steps. It might mean biting your tongue when you're tempted to snap, offering a kind word when it's least expected, or simply being present and listening. Grace also means setting healthy boundaries when needed, not out of resentment but out of love—for yourself and others.

If your family feels more chaotic than peaceful, remember that God is in the midst of it all. Pray for wisdom to handle conflicts, patience to endure challenges, and love to cover misunderstandings. Trust that He is working, even when it feels like nothing is changing.

God placed you in your family for a reason. Your role may be to be a peacemaker, an encourager, or simply a reflection of His love. And as you lean on Him, He will give you the strength to navigate the chaos with grace.

Prayer:

Lord, thank You for my family, with all its beauty and imperfections. Help me to love them as You love me, with grace, patience, and forgiveness. Give me wisdom to navigate challenges and courage to seek peace, even when it's difficult. Teach me to rely on Your strength and to trust that You are working in my family. Amen.

22

PRAYER MEETINGS: WHERE EVERYONE'S NOT-SO-SECRETLY JUDGING YOUR POTLUCK DISH

"For where two or three gather in my name, there am I with them." (Matthew 18:20, NIV)

Prayer meetings often bring a mix of feelings: joy, community, and... mild potluck anxiety. Will your casserole be a hit? Will your cookies be compared to someone else's perfectly baked ones? It's funny how something as small as a dish can overshadow the real reason we gather: to connect with God and with each other.

Matthew 18:20 reminds us that when two or three gather in Jesus' name, He is there with them. That's the heart of any prayer meeting—the promise of His presence. Yet, it's easy to let distractions, insecurities, or even minor tensions within the group shift our focus. Whether it's worrying about what others think of us or being preoccupied with the logistics, we can miss the opportunity to experience genuine connection with God and each other.

Prayer meetings are a gift. They're a chance to share burdens, celebrate victories, and stand together in faith. But like any gathering of imperfect people, they come with challenges. Maybe someone prays a little too long, or the conversation veers off topic. Maybe there's underlying tension between group members. These moments are opportunities to practice grace and to remember why we're there.

In the early church, believers gathered regularly to pray, break bread, and share life together (Acts 2:42-47). Their unity and devotion were so powerful that others were drawn to their faith. That same spirit of community is possible today, but it requires intentionality. It means focusing on God's presence rather than perfection. It means embracing differences and choosing love over judgment.

When we gather in prayer, we're reminded that we're not alone in our struggles. Sharing your heart and hearing someone else's story can bring encouragement and perspective. It's a chance to lift each other up and to witness how God is working in ways we might not see on our own.

So, the next time you find yourself at a prayer meeting, let go of the pressure to impress. Whether your potluck dish is a masterpiece or store-bought, it's not what matters. What matters is showing up with an open heart, ready to seek God and support others. Trust that He will use the gathering to strengthen your faith, deepen your relationships, and remind you of His presence.

And who knows? Maybe that casserole will be a hit after all.

Prayer:

Lord, thank You for the gift of community and for the promise of Your presence when we gather in Your name. Help me to approach prayer meetings with an open heart, focusing on You rather than distractions or insecurities. Teach me to extend grace to others and to value the connections You've placed in my life. Let our time together bring glory to You and encouragement to one another. Amen.

23

TRYING NOT TO JUDGE: EVERYONE'S GOT A LITTLE BIT OF CRAZY

"Do not judge, or you too will be judged." (Matthew 7:1, NIV)

Let's face it: judging others comes a little too naturally. We've all had those moments where we've raised an eyebrow at someone's behavior or silently thought, "I would never do that." But isn't it funny how, when we take a closer look, we all have our quirks and flaws? And if we're being *really* honest, none of us would appreciate someone else magnifying our imperfections under a judgmental lens.

In Matthew 7:1, Jesus makes it clear: judging others is not our job. It's a stern reminder that the same measure we use to judge others will be applied to us. Ouch. That verse hits hard because it highlights an uncomfortable truth: we often hold others to standards we struggle to meet ourselves. And while it's easy to notice the speck in someone else's eye, it takes humility and self-awareness to address the plank in our own.

Judgment stems from pride. It's the belief that we know better, that our way is the right way. But Scripture reminds us over and over that only God sees the whole picture. Only He knows the depths of someone's heart and the battles they're facing. When we judge, we're stepping into a role that belongs to Him alone.

So how do we stop the cycle of judgment? It starts with compassion. Instead of assuming the worst about someone, take a moment to consider what they might be going through. Maybe that coworker who's always short-tempered is carrying a heavy burden at home. Maybe the friend who seems distant is battling their own insecurities. When we approach others with empathy, judgment fades, and understanding takes its place.

Forgiveness also plays a key role. Often, judgment is fueled by unresolved hurt. When we're holding onto bitterness, it's easy to focus on someone else's flaws instead of addressing our own. But forgiveness frees us to love without barriers. It allows us to see others not as enemies, but as fellow humans in need of grace—just like us.

Finally, gratitude is a powerful antidote to judgment. When we're thankful for God's mercy in our own lives, it becomes easier to extend that same mercy to others. We're reminded that we're all works in progress, and that's okay. God isn't finished with any of us yet.

The truth is, we all have a little bit of crazy. We all fall short, make mistakes, and have moments we're not proud of. But God's grace covers it all. And as recipients of that grace, we're called to extend it to others. So the next time you're tempted to judge, pause and choose grace instead. You might just find that love and understanding go a lot further than criticism ever could.

Prayer:

Lord, thank You for Your grace that covers all my flaws and failures. Help me to extend that same grace to others and to resist the temptation to judge. Teach me to approach others with compassion and empathy, seeing them through Your eyes. Remind me of my own need for forgiveness and help me to reflect Your love in all I do. Amen.

24

SOCIAL MEDIA & SPIRITUAL WARFARE: SCROLLING WHILE SOUL SEARCHING

"Finally, be strong in the Lord and in His mighty power. Put on the full armor of God, so that you can take your stand against the devil's schemes."
(Ephesians 6:10-11, NIV)

Social media: a place where funny memes, highlight reels, and heated debates all coexist. It's a world we scroll through daily, often without realizing how it shapes our thoughts, emotions, and even our faith. While social media can be a tool for connection and inspiration, it can also become a battleground for spiritual warfare.

Ephesians 6:10-11 reminds us that we're not fighting against flesh and blood but against spiritual forces. And while this may sound dramatic in the context of your Instagram feed, think about it: how often does a casual scroll leave you feeling envious, anxious, or inadequate? The enemy is subtle, planting seeds of doubt and discontentment in the most seemingly harmless ways.

One of the biggest challenges of social media is comparison. You see someone else's perfectly curated life—their dream vacation, flawless family photos, or career milestones—and suddenly, your own blessings feel small. But here's the truth: those posts are only snapshots, not the full story. No one's life is as perfect as it looks online. God's plan for you is uniquely yours, and no amount of scrolling can diminish His purpose.

Social media can also distract us from what really matters. Hours spent scrolling can leave little time for prayer, Scripture, or meaningful connections. It's easy to justify it as harmless entertainment, but over time, it can dull our spiritual sensitivity. When we're constantly consuming content, we may miss the still, small voice of God.

So how do we navigate social media without losing our souls? First, approach it with intentionality. Before you open an app, ask yourself: Why am I here? Am I seeking inspiration, connection, or just killing time? Being mindful of your intentions can help you use social media as a tool rather than a trap.

Second, guard your heart. Proverbs 4:23 says, "Above all else, guard your heart, for everything you do flows from it." Be discerning about what you consume. If certain accounts or content make you feel envious, anxious, or angry, it's okay to unfollow or take a break. Fill your feed with things that uplift your spirit and point you toward God.

Finally, set boundaries. Limit your screen time and create space for God in your day. Instead of reaching for your phone first thing in the morning, start with prayer or Scripture. Replace mindless scrolling with intentional moments of gratitude or reflection. These small changes can make a big difference in keeping your heart and mind focused on what truly matters.

Social media isn't inherently bad, but it's a space where spiritual battles can occur. By staying rooted in God's truth and approaching it with wisdom, you can scroll without losing sight of your soul.

Prayer:

Lord, thank You for the tools and connections social media can provide. Help me to use it wisely and to guard my heart against comparison, distraction, and negativity. Teach me to stay grounded in Your truth and to find my worth in You, not in likes or followers. Guide my online interactions so they reflect Your love and light. Amen.

25

FINDING JOY: EVEN IN THE MUNDANE—LIKE CLEANING OUT YOUR FRIDGE

"Rejoice always, pray continually, give thanks in all circumstances; for this is God's will for you in Christ Jesus." (1 Thessalonians 5:16-18, NIV)

Let's be honest: cleaning out the fridge is not a task anyone gets excited about. It's messy, smelly, and often reveals forgotten leftovers that are better left unseen. Yet, there's something oddly satisfying about tackling the clutter and finding order amid the chaos. The fridge may not seem like a place to find joy, but it's a small example of how God can meet us in the mundane.

Paul's words in 1 Thessalonians 5:16-18 remind us to rejoice always, pray continually, and give thanks in all circumstances. Notice that this isn't conditional advice. It's not "rejoice when life is exciting" or "pray when you feel spiritual." It's a call to find joy, gratitude, and connection with God in every moment—even the mundane ones.

Life is full of ordinary tasks: folding laundry, running errands, mowing the lawn. These moments might not feel significant, but they're part of the rhythm of life God has given us. Finding joy in these moments doesn't mean pretending they're fun. It means shifting our perspective and inviting God into the process.

Consider how Jesus approached the mundane. During His ministry, He spent time doing everyday things: walking with His disciples, sharing meals, and attending weddings. Yet, in those moments, He revealed God's presence and purpose. The same can be true for us. When we approach our daily tasks with gratitude and awareness of God's presence, they become opportunities for worship and growth.

Finding joy in the mundane also requires us to let go of perfection. That fridge you just cleaned will get messy again. The laundry will pile up, and the to-do list will grow. But joy isn't about achieving perfect order; it's about embracing the process and trusting that God is at work, even in the small things.

Gratitude is the gateway to joy. Instead of grumbling about the chores, thank God for the home you have to clean, the food you have to store, and the hands that can do the work. These simple shifts in perspective can transform a mundane task into a moment of worship.

The next time you find yourself in the middle of an ordinary chore, pause and invite God into the moment. Pray while you work. Reflect on His goodness. Choose to see the task as an opportunity to practice gratitude and find joy. You might just discover that even the most routine parts of life are filled with His presence.

Prayer:

Lord, thank You for being present in every moment, even the mundane ones. Help me to find joy in the ordinary tasks of life and to approach them with gratitude. Teach me to see Your hand in all things and to worship You through the rhythm of my day. Thank You for the blessings You've given me, and remind me to rejoice always, knowing that You are with me. Amen.

26

ON THE ROAD TO PATIENCE: AVOIDING THE RUMBLE STRIPS OF LIFE

"Be completely humble and gentle; be patient, bearing with one another in love." (Ephesians 4:2, NIV)

Patience is like driving on a long stretch of highway. The road seems endless, the destination far off, and the rumble strips serve as a jarring reminder when you veer off course. Whether it's waiting in line, dealing with slow drivers, or navigating a season of unanswered prayers, patience can feel like a test we didn't sign up for.

Ephesians 4:2 calls us to be humble, gentle, and patient, bearing with one another in love. These aren't just pleasant suggestions; they're essential for maintaining harmony with others and growing in our faith. But let's be honest: patience is hard. It's not something that comes naturally to most of us, especially in a world that thrives on instant gratification.

Patience, however, isn't just about enduring delays or frustrations. It's about trusting God's timing and allowing Him to work in ways we can't yet see. Think about Joseph in the

Bible. He endured years of slavery and imprisonment before stepping into the role God had prepared for him. In those long, difficult years, Joseph could have given up. Instead, he trusted that God was working behind the scenes, even when the road ahead seemed uncertain.

When we're tempted to lose patience, it's helpful to remember that God is patient with us. How many times have we fallen short, yet He remains steadfast, guiding us with grace? His patience is an example for us to follow. It's a reminder that patience isn't passive; it's active trust in God's plan.

Avoiding the rumble strips of impatience requires intentional effort. Start by recognizing the triggers that test your patience. Is it a coworker's slow responses, a child's endless questions, or a season of waiting for an answered prayer? Identifying these moments allows you to pause and respond with grace instead of frustration.

Prayer is another powerful tool. When you feel impatience rising, take a moment to breathe and pray. Ask God for the strength to endure and the wisdom to trust His timing. Philippians 4:6-7 reminds us to bring our anxieties to God in prayer, promising that His peace will guard our hearts and minds.

Finally, practice gratitude. It's hard to be impatient when you're focused on the blessings in front of you. Thank God for the opportunities to grow, the people in your life, and the lessons learned along the way. Gratitude shifts our perspective from frustration to faith.

As you journey on the road to patience, remember that God is with you every step of the way. The process may be uncomfortable at times, but it's shaping you into the person He's called you to be. Trust that His timing is perfect, and let patience have its perfect work in your life.

Prayer:

Lord, thank You for Your patience with me. Teach me to reflect that patience in my interactions with others and in the situations that test my endurance. Help me to trust Your timing and to find peace in the waiting. Remind me that every delay and challenge is an opportunity to grow closer to You. Amen.

27

WHEN LIFE GIVES YOU LEMONS: MAKE A DIVINE LEMONADE STAND!

"And we know that in all things God works for the good of those who love Him, who have been called according to His purpose." (Romans 8:28, NIV)

Life has a funny way of throwing us curveballs. Sometimes, they come in the form of unexpected challenges, disappointments, or setbacks that leave us questioning, "Why is this happening?" It's easy to feel bitter when life gives us lemons, but Romans 8:28 reminds us that God can use every situation—even the sour ones—for our good and His purpose.

Think about the process of making lemonade. You take something sour and unpleasant, mix in a little sweetness, and create something refreshing. Similarly, God takes the sour moments of our lives and, with His grace and wisdom, turns them into something beautiful. The key is allowing Him to work and trusting that His plan is greater than what we can see in the moment.

Consider the story of Esther. She found herself in a situation she didn't ask for—living in a foreign palace and thrust into the role of queen during a time of great danger for her people. Yet, through God's providence, she used her position to save her nation. What could have been a story of bitterness became one of triumph because Esther trusted God and stepped into her purpose.

When life gives us lemons, our natural instinct might be to complain or focus on the bitterness. But what if we saw those lemons as opportunities? Every challenge is a chance to grow, to rely on God, and to witness His transforming power. That difficult job? It might be teaching you perseverance. That strained relationship? It could be refining your ability to love and forgive. That unexpected detour? It might be leading you to a blessing you never imagined.

The sweetness in our lemonade comes from gratitude and faith. Gratitude shifts our focus from what we've lost to what we've gained. Faith reminds us that God is in control, even when life feels chaotic. Together, they create a perspective that sees challenges not as obstacles but as opportunities for God to work.

So, the next time life hands you a batch of lemons, don't let them sour your spirit. Bring them to God and let Him show you how to make lemonade. Trust that He is working behind the scenes, using every moment to shape you and fulfill His purpose. And as you step forward in faith, you'll discover that even the most bitter situations can become sweet testimonies of His goodness.

Prayer:

Lord, thank You for working in all things, even the difficult and unexpected moments. Help me to trust Your plan and to see challenges as opportunities to grow closer to You. Teach me to approach life with gratitude and faith, knowing that You can turn every sour situation into something beautiful. Thank You for Your constant presence and love. Amen.

28

THE GIFT OF TONGUE: USING YOUR WORDS WISELY (AND SOMETIMES SILLY)

"The tongue has the power of life and death, and those who love it will eat its fruit." (Proverbs 18:21, NIV)

Words are powerful. With a few sentences, you can build someone up, tear someone down, or simply leave them confused if you're trying out a new pun. The gift of language is one of God's greatest blessings, but like any gift, it comes with responsibility. Proverbs 18:21 reminds us that the tongue has the power of life and death. That's no small thing. Every word we speak carries weight, whether we realize it or not.

Think about the conversations you've had recently. Did your words encourage and uplift? Or were they laced with impatience, gossip, or negativity? It's easy to let our tongues run wild, especially when we're frustrated or distracted. But the Bible calls us to something higher. James 3:9-10 challenges us, saying, "With the tongue, we praise our Lord and Father, and with it we curse human beings, who have been made in God's likeness. Out of the same mouth come praise and cursing. My brothers and sisters, this should not be." (NIV)

Our words are a reflection of our hearts. Jesus said in Matthew 12:34, "For the mouth speaks what the heart is full of." If our words are often harsh or careless, it's a sign that we need to invite God to do some heart work. He can help us cultivate kindness, patience, and love so that what flows from our lips honors Him and blesses others.

But using our words wisely doesn't mean we have to be serious all the time. There's room for humor, silliness, and lighthearted conversations that bring joy. Laughter is a gift from God, and when we share it with others, it's a way of reflecting His joy. The key is to ensure that even our jokes and playful words are kind and considerate.

One practical way to use your words wisely is to pause before speaking. Ask yourself: Is what I'm about to say true? Is it kind? Is it necessary? These simple questions can prevent a lot of unnecessary hurt and help us speak life into the people around us. Another way is to use your words intentionally to encourage and build up others. A simple "Thank you," "I appreciate you," or "You're doing a great job" can go a long way.

Remember, words are seeds. The ones you plant today will bear fruit tomorrow. Choose to plant seeds of love, grace, and encouragement. And when you stumble—because we all do—ask for forgiveness and strive to do better. God's grace is big enough to cover our mistakes and guide us toward growth.

So, use your words wisely, whether you're comforting a friend, making someone laugh, or praising God in prayer. Speak life, and watch how God uses your words to bless others and glorify Him.

Prayer:

Lord, thank You for the gift of words and the ability to communicate. Help me to use my tongue wisely, to speak life and encouragement, and to reflect Your love in everything I say. Guard my heart so that my words flow from a place of grace and truth. Teach me to bring joy and healing through my speech and to honor You in every conversation. Amen.

29

DOUBTING THOMAS: THE APOSTLE WITH TRUST ISSUES— RELATABLE, RIGHT?

"Then Jesus told him, 'Because you have seen me, you have believed; blessed are those who have not seen and yet have believed.'" (John 20:29, NIV)

We've all had moments of doubt. Whether it's questioning God's plans, wondering if He hears our prayers, or simply struggling to believe in His promises, doubt is a natural part of the faith journey. And if there's one biblical figure who embodies this struggle, it's Thomas.

Thomas, one of Jesus' twelve disciples, is often remembered for one thing: doubting. After Jesus' resurrection, He appeared to the disciples, but Thomas wasn't there. When the others told him they had seen the Lord, Thomas famously replied, "Unless I see the nail marks in His hands and put my finger where the nails were, and put my hand into His side, I will not believe" (John 20:25, NIV).

Can you blame him? The idea of someone rising from the dead defies all logic and reason. Thomas wasn't being malicious; he was being honest. He wanted proof—something tangible to confirm what sounded impossible. And isn't that what we often want? When life feels uncertain, when prayers go unanswered, or when God seems silent, we long for reassurance, for a sign that He's still there.

The beautiful thing about Thomas' story is how Jesus responds. Eight days later, Jesus appears again, this time with Thomas present. He doesn't scold Thomas for his doubts. Instead, He invites him to touch His wounds and see for himself. "Stop doubting and believe," Jesus says (John 20:27, NIV). Thomas' response is immediate: "My Lord and my God!" (John 20:28, NIV).

Jesus' gentle response to Thomas shows us that doubt isn't the end of faith. It's often the beginning of a deeper relationship with Him. God isn't threatened by our questions or uncertainties. He meets us in our doubts, offering His presence and peace.

If you're wrestling with doubt today, take heart. You're not alone, and your doubts don't disqualify you from God's love or His plans. Instead of running from your questions, bring them to God. Pray honestly, just as Thomas spoke honestly. Search His Word for truth, and surround yourself with others who can encourage your faith.

Faith doesn't mean having all the answers. It means trusting God even when we don't. Jesus said, "Blessed are those who have not seen and yet have believed" (John 20:29, NIV). That's you and me. We may not have seen Jesus' physical wounds, but we have His promises, His Spirit, and His love to sustain us.

So, the next time doubt creeps in, remember Thomas. Remember that Jesus met him in his uncertainty and led him to belief. And trust that He will do the same for you.

Prayer:

Lord, thank You for meeting me in my doubts and for loving me through my questions. Help me to trust You even when I don't have all the answers. Strengthen my faith and remind me of Your promises. Thank You for being patient with me and for guiding me closer to You. Amen.

30

GRINNING IN THE GLOOM: FINDING GOD'S LIGHT IN YOUR DARKEST MOMENTS

"The light shines in the darkness, and the darkness has not overcome it." (John 1:5, NIV)

Darkness has a way of making everything feel heavier. Whether it's the weight of grief, the sting of disappointment, or the uncertainty of the future, life's darker seasons can leave us feeling overwhelmed and alone. But as John 1:5 reminds us, God's light shines in the darkness, and no amount of gloom can extinguish it.

In our hardest moments, it can be difficult to see God's hand at work. Questions arise: "Why is this happening?" "Where are You, Lord?" Yet, the Bible is filled with stories of God's presence in the midst of despair. Think of Paul and Silas, sitting in a dark prison cell after being beaten and humiliated. Instead of succumbing to despair, they prayed and sang hymns (Acts 16:25). Their worship in the gloom became a powerful testimony of God's faithfulness, and it ultimately led to their freedom.

85

Darkness doesn't mean God is absent. In fact, it's often where His light shines the brightest. Psalm 34:18 assures us, "The Lord is close to the brokenhearted and saves those who are crushed in spirit" (NIV). When we feel the weight of life pressing down, God draws near, offering comfort, strength, and hope.

Finding joy in the gloom doesn't mean pretending everything is fine. It means acknowledging the pain while choosing to trust in God's promises. It's about looking for the small glimmers of His presence—a kind word from a friend, a song that speaks to your heart, or a sunrise that reminds you of His faithfulness. These moments may not erase the darkness, but they remind us that we're not alone.

Joy in hard times also comes from gratitude. Even in the most challenging seasons, there's always something to be thankful for. Gratitude shifts our focus from what we've lost to what we still have, from the shadows to the light. And as we give thanks, we open our hearts to God's peace, which transcends all understanding (Philippians 4:6-7).

If you're walking through a dark season, take heart. The same God who led His people through the wilderness, who calmed the storm for His disciples, and who raised Jesus from the dead is with you. His light is stronger than any darkness you face. Lean into Him, let His Word guide you, and trust that He is working all things for your good (Romans 8:28).

Darkness doesn't have the final say. God's light does. And when you look to Him, you'll find not only the strength to endure but also the joy to grin in the gloom, knowing that His love never fails.

Prayer:

Lord, thank You for being my light in the darkest moments of life. Help me to trust in Your presence and to see the glimmers of Your goodness even when the path feels uncertain. Fill my heart with gratitude and remind me that Your light can never be overcome. Strengthen my faith and guide me closer to You each day. Amen.

www.ingramcontent.com/pod-product-compliance
Lightning Source LLC
Chambersburg PA
CBHW010937120626
46554CB00007B/2501